WELCOME TO RYAN'S WORLD!

Ready-to-Read

Simon Spotlight
New York   London   Toronto   Sydney   New Delhi

SIMON SPOTLIGHT
An imprint of Simon & Schuster Children's Publishing Division
1230 Avenue of the Americas, New York, New York 10020
This Simon Spotlight edition July 2019
Text by May Nakamura
TM & © 2019 RTR Production, LLC, RFR Entertainment, Inc. and Remka, Inc., and PocketWatch, Inc. Ryan ToysReview,
Ryan's World and all related titles, logos and characters are trademarks of RTR Production, LLC, RFR Entertainment, Inc.
and Remka, Inc. The pocket.watch logo and all related titles, logos, and characters are trademarks of PocketWatch, Inc.
All Rights Reserved. • Photos and illustrations of Ryan's World characters copyright © 2019 RTR Production, LLC, RFR
Entertainment, Inc., and Remka, Inc.
Stock photos copyright © iStock.com. • All rights reserved, including the right of reproduction in whole or in part in any form.
SIMON SPOTLIGHT, READY-TO-READ, and colophon are registered trademarks of Simon & Schuster, Inc.
For information about special discounts for bulk purchases, please contact Simon & Schuster Special Sales at 1-866-506-1949
or business@simonandschuster.com.
Manufactured in the United States of America 0321 LAK
6 8 10 9 7 5
ISBN 978-1-5344-4077-7 (hc)
ISBN 978-1-5344-4076-0 (pbk)
ISBN 978-1-5344-4078-4 (eBook)

Hi, I am Ryan!

I am seven years old.

I like playing with toys and making videos.

Do you want to visit?

Follow me!

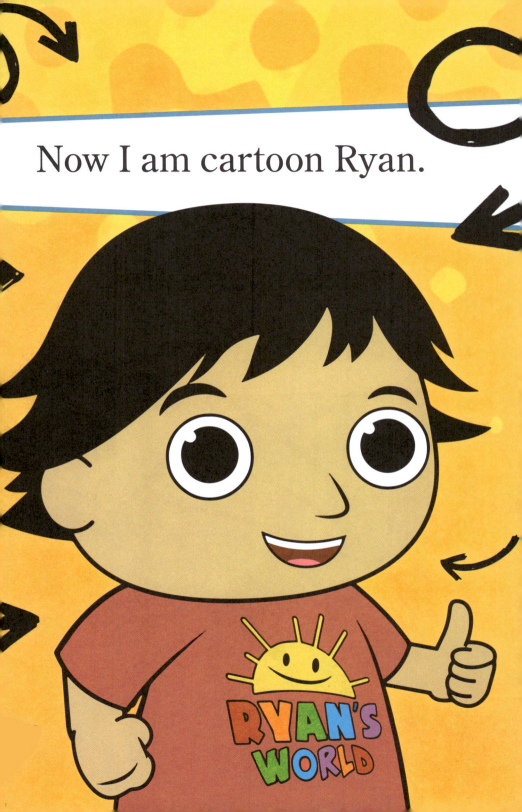

In my world, there are so many ways to play! We can play sports. My favorite sports are soccer and tennis.

I also like riding my skateboard and playing football.

We can drive around like a race car driver.

We can also play video games. When I grow up, I want to make my own games!

In my world,
we can be anything.
We can pretend
to be pirates!

We can pretend to travel to space.

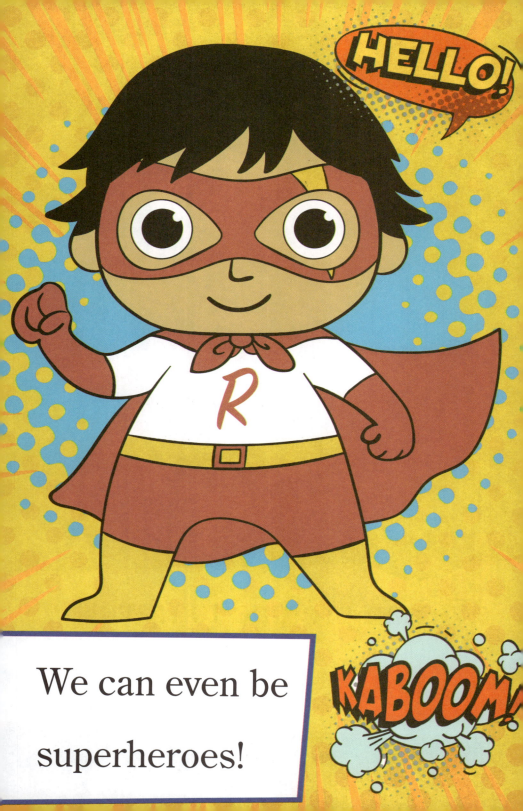

My superhero name is Red Titan.

As Red Titan, I am super strong!

I am getting hungry.

Let's eat pizza!

It is my favorite food.

Here is a whole pizza just for you!

What is your favorite pizza topping?

Now that we have eaten, let's meet my friends.

This is Peck the penguin.

He likes science.

I do too!

This is Gus
the Gummy Gator.
He loves eating
yummy gummies.
Gus and his friend Moe
like exploring together.

Once I ate the largest gummy worm in the world. It was super sweet . . . and yummy!

This is Alpha Lexa. She loves fashion and trying on new clothes.

Gil lives in the ocean.

He likes to swim with his fish friends.

Combo Panda is not home.

I wonder where he is.

Look!

It is a mystery egg.

I like opening mystery eggs in my videos. What do you think is inside?

The egg is starting to shake!

Wow!

Combo Panda

was hiding inside!

He is so silly!

I am glad you got to meet Combo Panda.

Now it is time to go home.

Thanks for visiting

Ryan's World!

Come visit me again soon!